T0144019

BYE-BYE NANNY

(Based on a True Story)

MIRIAM CLAIRE

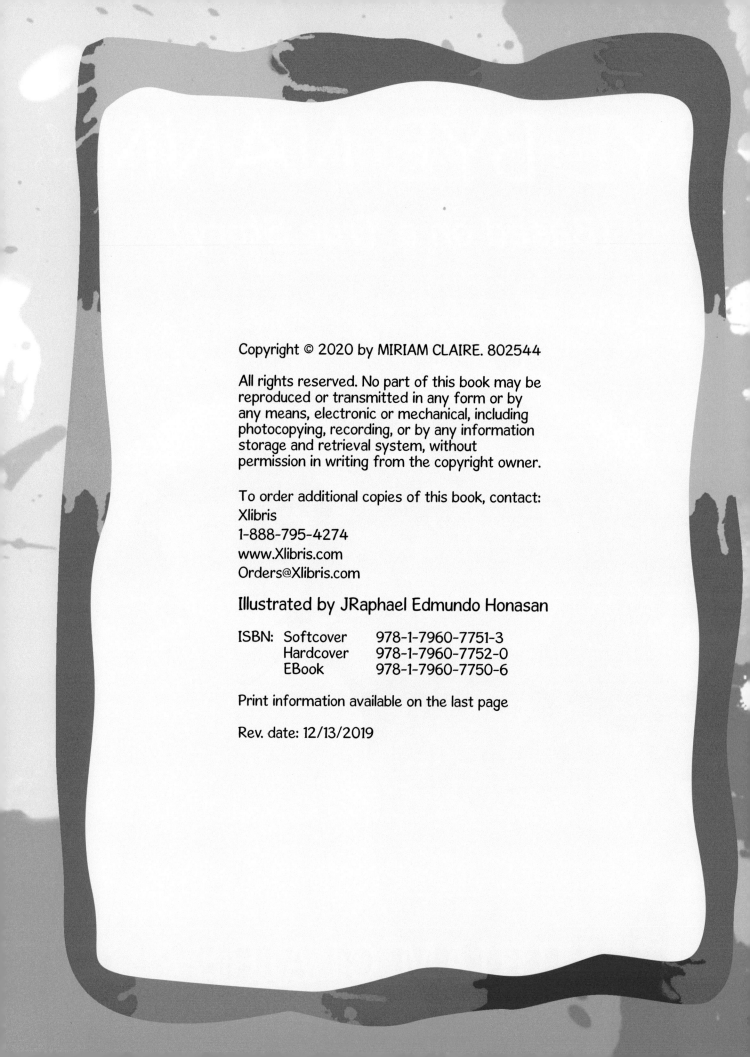

Copyright © 2020 by MIRIAM CLAIRE. 802544

All rights reserved. No part of this book may be
reproduced or transmitted in any form or by
any means, electronic or mechanical, including
photocopying, recording, or by any information
storage and retrieval system, without
permission in writing from the copyright owner.

To order additional copies of this book, contact:
Xlibris
1-888-795-4274
www.Xlibris.com
Orders@Xlibris.com

Illustrated by JRaphael Edmundo Honasan

ISBN: Softcover   978-1-7960-7751-3
       Hardcover   978-1-7960-7752-0
       EBook   978-1-7960-7750-6

Print information available on the last page

Rev. date: 12/13/2019

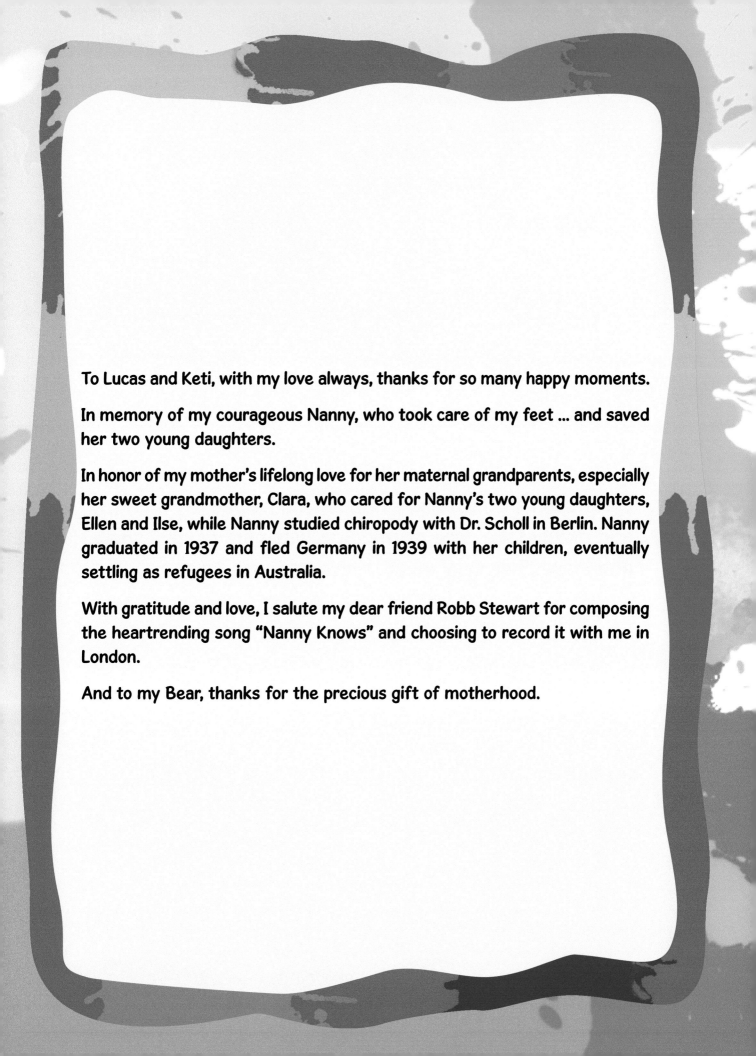

To Lucas and Keti, with my love always, thanks for so many happy moments.

In memory of my courageous Nanny, who took care of my feet … and saved her two young daughters.

In honor of my mother's lifelong love for her maternal grandparents, especially her sweet grandmother, Clara, who cared for Nanny's two young daughters, Ellen and Ilse, while Nanny studied chiropody with Dr. Scholl in Berlin. Nanny graduated in 1937 and fled Germany in 1939 with her children, eventually settling as refugees in Australia.

With gratitude and love, I salute my dear friend Robb Stewart for composing the heartrending song "Nanny Knows" and choosing to record it with me in London.

And to my Bear, thanks for the precious gift of motherhood.

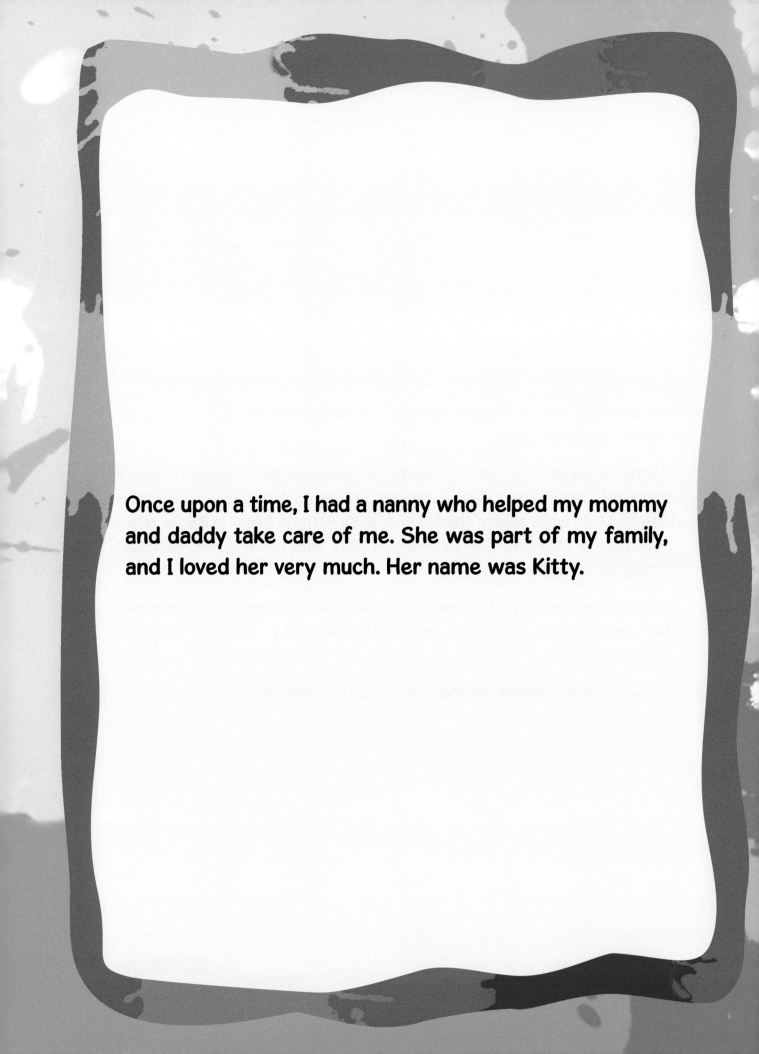

Once upon a time, I had a nanny who helped my mommy and daddy take care of me. She was part of my family, and I loved her very much. Her name was Kitty.

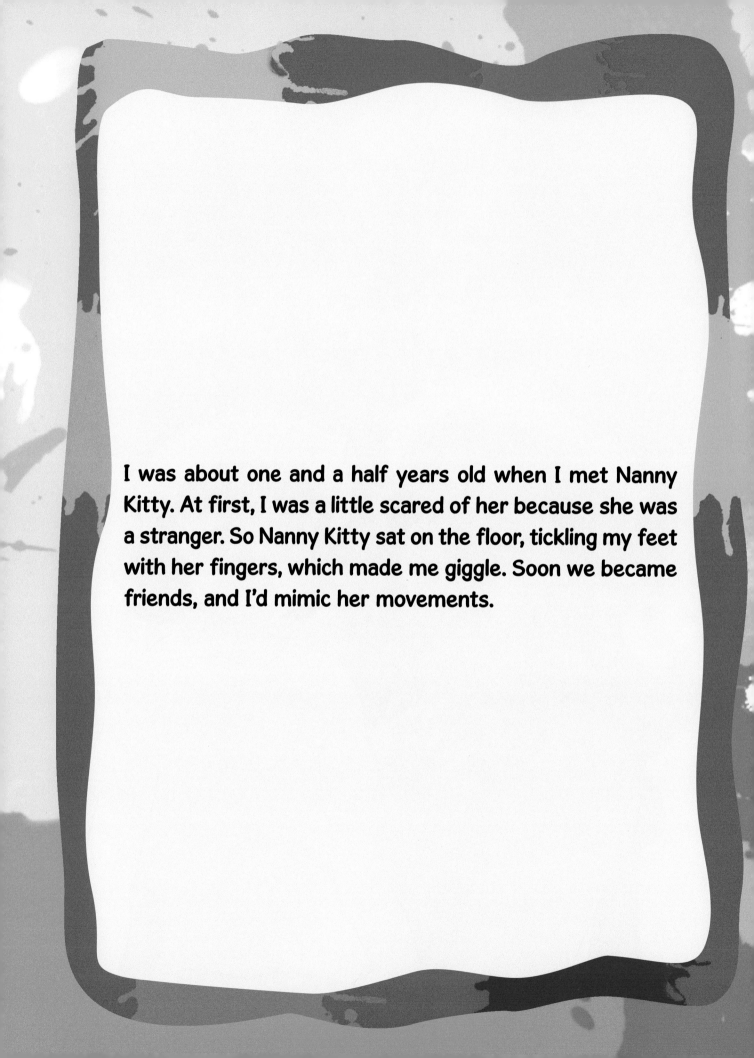

I was about one and a half years old when I met Nanny Kitty. At first, I was a little scared of her because she was a stranger. So Nanny Kitty sat on the floor, tickling my feet with her fingers, which made me giggle. Soon we became friends, and I'd mimic her movements.

Nanny Kitty played lots of fun games with me. My favorite was dinosaur fighting, because we'd wrestle during the battle. I often asked Nanny Kitty to watch my favorite dinosaur fight in Walt Disney's movie *Fantasia*, and then we'd act out the whole scene.

My second most favorite game was pretending that I was a magician. To make Nanny Kitty disappear, I'd bury her under all the fuzzy animals in my nursery. Then I'd make her magically reappear by throwing the fuzzy animals off her. To celebrate my successful trick, I'd sit on Nanny Kitty's back, and she would take me for a ride.

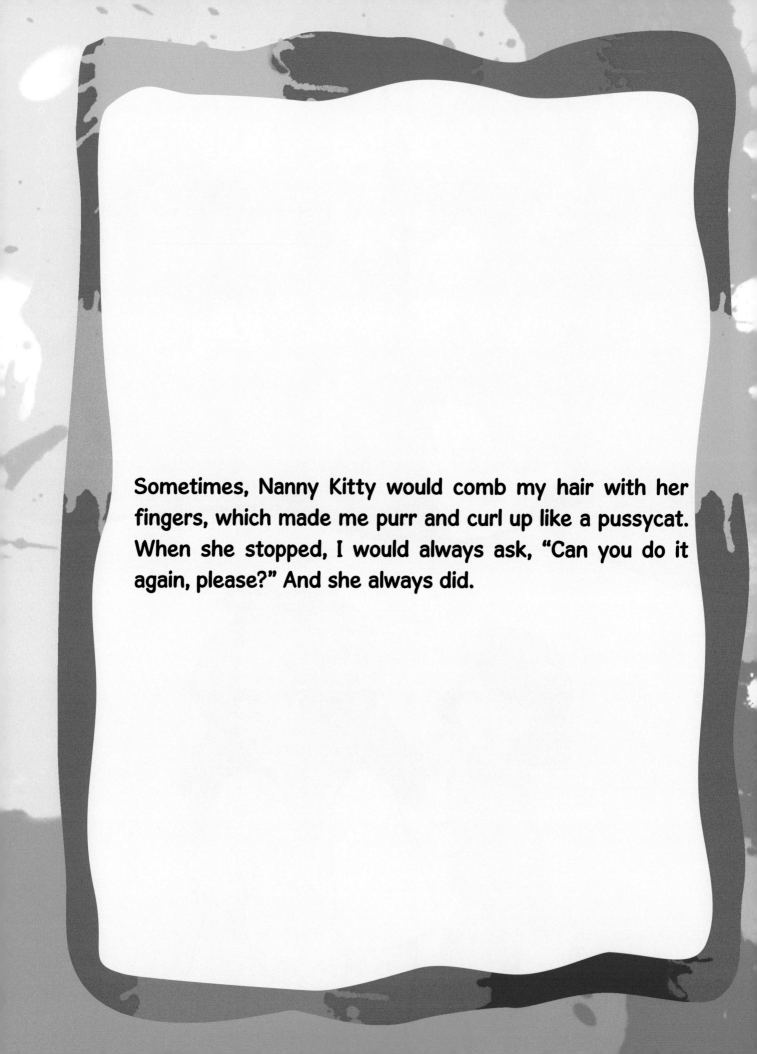

Sometimes, Nanny Kitty would comb my hair with her fingers, which made me purr and curl up like a pussycat. When she stopped, I would always ask, "Can you do it again, please?" And she always did.

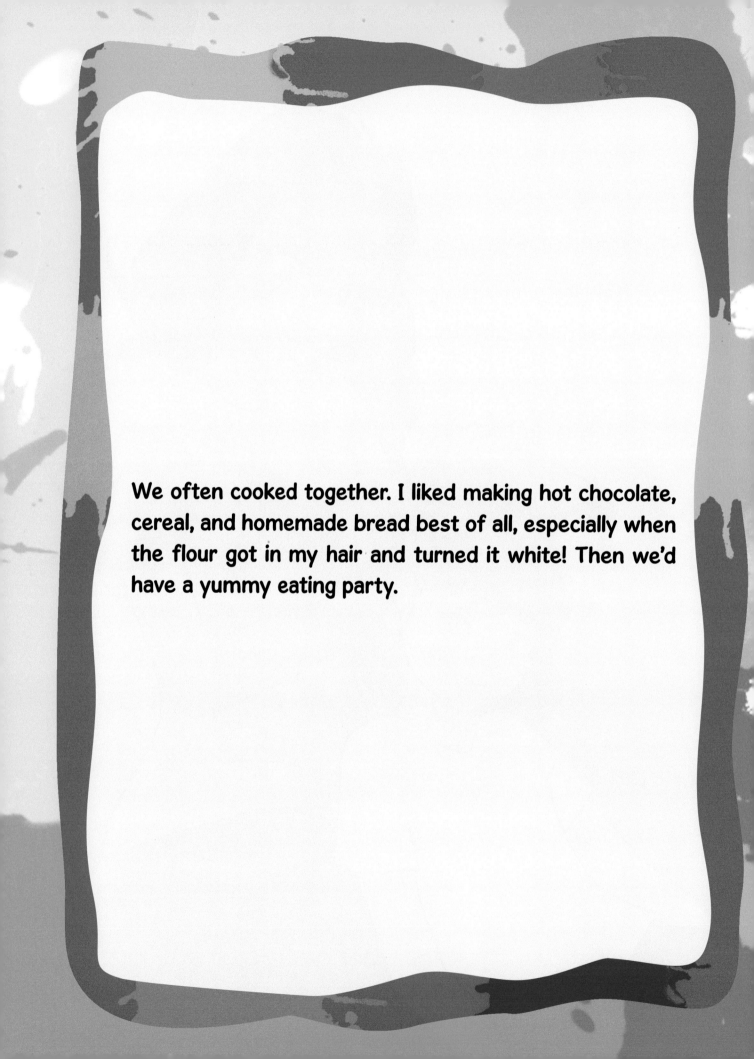

We often cooked together. I liked making hot chocolate, cereal, and homemade bread best of all, especially when the flour got in my hair and turned it white! Then we'd have a yummy eating party.

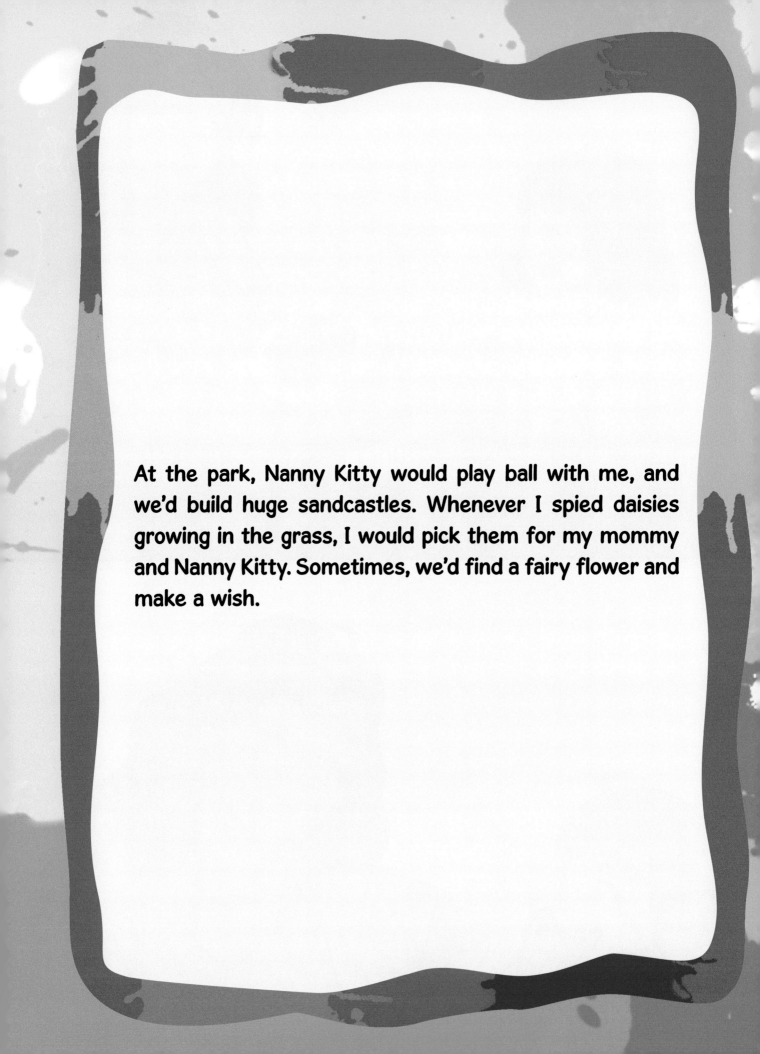

At the park, Nanny Kitty would play ball with me, and we'd build huge sandcastles. Whenever I spied daisies growing in the grass, I would pick them for my mommy and Nanny Kitty. Sometimes, we'd find a fairy flower and make a wish.

In our garden, Nanny Kitty would follow me around while I waved my magic water wand, painting rain pictures in the air. The plants perked up and grew when I watered them. Somehow, I always seemed to get wet too. Maybe that's why I've grown so much.

When I took a bath, Nanny Kitty would say, "Let's go fishing," and we'd take out our fishing rods to catch colored fish.

If I were sick, Nanny Kitty would bring me a hot-water bottle to cuddle and read me a story. Sometimes, she would hum the "Nighty Night" song that my mommy sings to me at bedtime to make me feel better. If Nanny Kitty felt sick, I would give her an apple along with a cold hot-water bottle to cuddle, and then I'd try to sing the "Nighty Night" song to make her feel better.

Every now and then, Nanny Kitty and I would argue, usually because we couldn't agree on what to do next. When I was tired, I wasn't a very good listener, and I would insist on doing something that Nanny Kitty didn't want me to do. Mommy would come to rescue us from my crossness and tell me that it was nap time. Nanny Kitty and I were always best friends again after my nap.

One day, Nanny Kitty told me that she couldn't be my nanny anymore. "Why?" I asked. "Who will take care of me when Mommy and Daddy can't be with me? Did I do something wrong? Don't you like me anymore?" Nanny Kitty explained that she had to fly away on an airplane to another country for a whole year to study.

"Of course you haven't done anything wrong," she said. "I love you and will miss you very much. Mommy and Daddy will find someone else to take care of you while I'm away. Please try to be happy for me, even if you feel sad that I'm going away. Studying in another country is something that I've always wanted to do, so this is a dream come true for me."

I couldn't imagine what life would be like without Nanny Kitty. I felt sad at first, and then I got angry at her for going away, even though she wasn't gone yet.

When the day finally arrived for her to fly away, we had a going-away party and ate an airplane-shaped ice cream cake with a "Good luck" candle in it. I sang her a special song, "Happy Bye-Bye to You," but when she went to leave, I refused to say goodbye. I thought that maybe if I didn't say goodbye, she wouldn't go. It didn't work. Nanny Kitty gave me a big kiss and hug, promised to write, and then waved as she walked through our door. I waved back and blew her a sad kiss. I'd said bye-bye to her every day when she left to go home, but now that she was going away for a whole year, the words seemed to have a different meaning.

While Nanny Kitty was away, I couldn't wait for the mailman to deliver the mail. Every now and then, he'd deliver a postcard from Nanny Kitty, and I'd jump up and down with glee. She remembered me and missed me and loved me, even though she was far away.

Once, she sent me an email letter. It arrived on my mommy's computer!

On Nanny Kitty's birthday, we phoned her and sang "Happy Birthday to You." Hearing the sound of her voice on the phone was wonderful, because she didn't seem so far away. And on my birthday, we phoned her again to say thank you for the presents she sent me in the mail. Nanny Kitty sang to me, and I cried happy tears.

One day, when I was missing Nanny Kitty really badly, I started writing letters to her. I'd draw a picture or write something I wanted to tell her, put the piece of paper in an envelope addressed to Nanny Kitty, stick a stamp on it, and then mail it in a postbox. That made me feel better. Once, I even sent her an email letter on Mommy's computer, along with a picture of me!

When Nanny Kitty returned, we had a wonderful "hello" party. Waving hello was much more fun than waving bye-bye when she left. I gave her a balloon that said, "Welcome Home," and Nanny Kitty gave me a present. It was a sweater with words on it that said, "The person who gave me this sweater loves me very much."

While Nanny Kitty worked as my nanny, she was studying at university to become an elementary school teacher. When she returned home from studying in another country, she went back to university and continued being my nanny until we moved to a different city. We shared many happy times together.

When we moved, my mommy changed jobs so that she and Daddy could take care of me without the help of a nanny. By that time, I was in kindergarten. Saying bye-bye to Nanny Kitty when we moved made me cry. I knew that I would miss her terribly. Nanny Kitty promised to come for a sleepover visit to our new home, and she did. I was so happy to see her. We had a dinosaur fight as soon as she arrived. When she left to go home the next day, I said, "Bye-bye Nanny Kitty," but this time, I didn't feel sad or cry because I knew that I'd see her again.

Nanny Kitty will always be part of my family, even when she's not with me.

During the year that Nanny Kitty was away, six other nannies came to look after me and play with me. Mommy and Daddy had to fire Nanny no. 1 because she let me run out on the road in front of our home, where cars drive. I was not allowed to be on the road without holding the hand of a grown-up whom I knew. I didn't really like Nanny no. 1 very much, so saying bye-bye to her was easy.

Nanny no. 2 was nice, but she got married and moved to a new home that was too far away for her to drive to see me. Saying bye-bye to her was pretty easy too because I hadn't known her very long.

When Nanny no. 3 had to leave, the bye-bye was sad because she got sick and didn't have enough energy to run around with me anymore. I said "I hope you get well soon" when she left and gave her a kiss to make her feel better.

Mommy and Daddy had to send Nanny no. 4 away because she took something from our home that didn't belong to her. I wondered why. Maybe she needed it, I thought, but Daddy said that even if she needed what she took, it wasn't okay for her to take it without asking first. I didn't get a chance to say bye-bye to her, but that's okay, because I know that it wasn't my fault that she left. I hope in my heart that she gets what she needs one day.

The case of Nanny no. 5 is still a mystery, because she left without saying bye-bye. One day, she just didn't show up. Her disappearance left me feeling frustrated and incomplete, like when I lost a piece of a jigsaw puzzle. Did she leave because she didn't like me? Did I do something wrong? Did she get sick, lost, injured, or called home for a family emergency? Maybe she suddenly wanted a vacation? Sometimes, I imagine saying bye-bye to her and wonder if she will ever come back.

The first day that I met Nanny no. 6, I loved playing ball with her, but the next day, she lost her temper when I slipped and almost fell into the swimming pool. She shouted at me and smacked my hand, which made me cry. My mommy saw what happened and told Nanny no. 6 that she didn't feel comfortable with her watching over me. Mommy said that in our house, if a child falls you ask "Did you hurt yourself?" and help her get up for a hug and kiss on the boo-boo. If I did something wrong, then I could be sent to my room to think about it. Nannies in our house are not allowed to hit me. That bye-bye made me feel relieved because I knew that when Nanny no. 6 walked out the door, she would never be coming back.

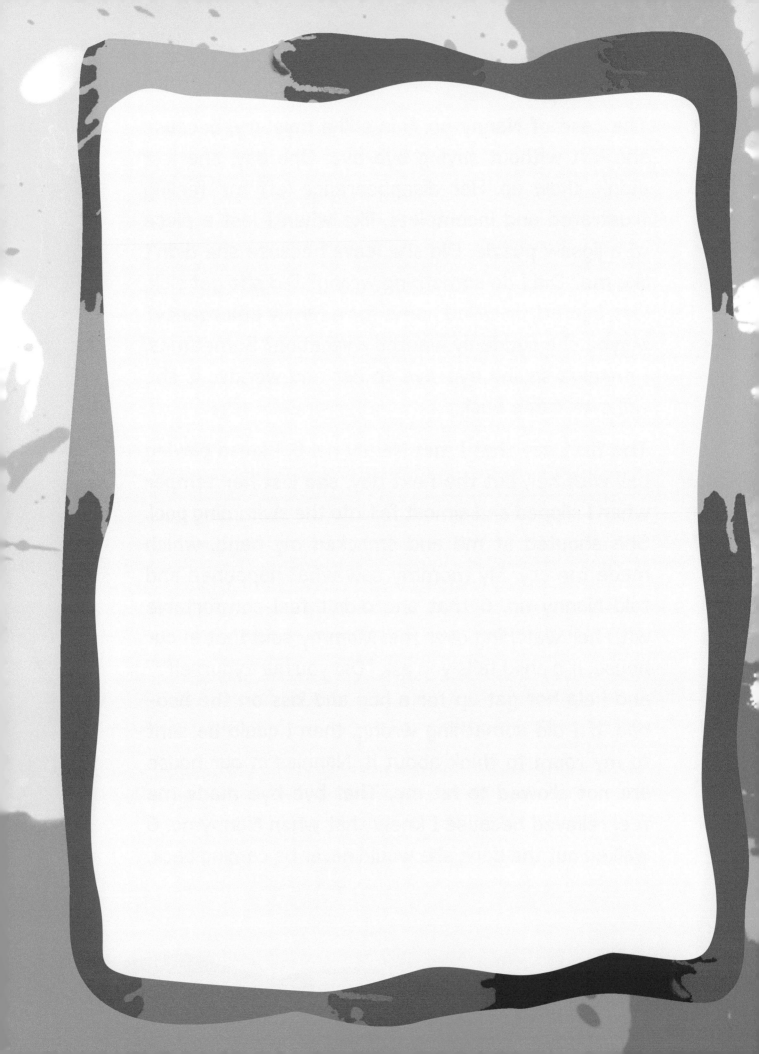

Dear Parents,

Bye-Bye Nanny is based on our experience with my son, Lucas, and his nanny, Aketa. Lucas could not pronounce Aketa's name properly and would call her Keti or Kitty.

While swapping nanny stories with other parents, I realized just how lucky we were to find our Kitty, who worked for us for over five years, on and off. She became part of our family. We also found other nannies who worked for us for a short time or shared the nannying job with Kitty when she was busy at college, by advertising in the local university newspaper or through a nanny agency.

Another nanny, Kema, who was pregnant while she worked for us, has since had her baby. We remained friends with Kema and her family. The story of how we met Kema is truly remarkable. After driving the nanny who let my son run out on the road to her bus on the last day that she worked for us, Lucas and I went to the park for a second time, which was unusual. I was at a loss to figure out how to find another nanny at short notice. When we arrived, Kema, who was a complete stranger, walked up to us and said, "Do you know anyone who needs a nanny?"

The coincidence was so unbelievable that I set up an appointment to meet her again, and things worked out.

One mother, Nancy, recalled how she cried, desperately trying to think how she would explain to her three-year-old son that his nanny had disappeared without saying goodbye to him. He loved her. (The nanny eventually had a friend call to say that she wouldn't be coming back to work and gave no reason for her abrupt departure after two years working as the child's nanny.) Nancy decided to buy gifts and a goodbye card and present them to her son as gifts from his nanny. The card from the nanny told him that she loved him and was sorry that she had to leave so suddenly. She explained that she was going to see her family in another country. Her son was happy to receive the gifts and card from his beloved nanny. The next day, his mother cried again, thinking about how uncaring the nanny had been to leave without giving notice or saying goodbye. Her son caught her crying and asked why. When she said that she was sad because his nanny had left so suddenly, he responded thus, "Why are you sad? You should be happy for her because she's gone to be with her family." While I'm a firm believer in telling children edited truth, I must say that Nancy's way of dealing with the sudden disappearance of her son's nanny seems perfect. She can always tell him the truth when he's twenty-one.

The following nanny horror stories all led to nannies leaving without saying goodbye. Somehow, parents have to figure out how to explain the rather extraordinary behavior of nannies who get fired or disappear for bizarre reasons, like stealing, giving a child medicine without parental permission in order to get the child to go to sleep early, child abuse, arson, a pay dispute, and locking a child in a closet as punishment, to name just a few.

I hope this book helps you and your child cope with saying "bye-bye Nanny."

Reflections on *Bye-Bye Nanny* by the real Nanny Kitty

Reading *Bye-Bye Nanny* brought back so many wonderful and happy memories. As I made the trip down memory lane, I realized how important that time was for me as a young adult in college and as an aspiring classroom teacher. Moreover, now that I am a mother, I can see how my experience as Lucas's nanny shaped my understanding of family and motherhood.

When I began my nanny job, I was still in college. College presented many ups and downs in life, and it was, of course, at times too draining and serious. But taking care of Lucas was my safe haven. It was my time to be in a world that was free of student responsibilities. I had to be truly present to enter Lucas's world of music, dinosaurs, magic water hoses, and gardens!

Watching Lucas develop his love of music taught me an important lesson about working with children as a teacher and a mother. There is no one size fits all in learning and success in life. Every child is unique and has a passion. As teachers, parents, and caregivers, it is our role to help nurture the natural curiosity and interests of our children so that they can uncover their true passions in life. It is through this meaningful pursuit that our children experience fulfillment and happiness.

In addition, the experience caring for Lucas and being included in his life with his mom and dad taught me that family is more than just a blood relationship. We are family when we share joys and sorrows. We are family when we share celebrations and misfortunes. We are family when we share love. To this day, I share this special love with Lucas. In my heart and in his, I will always be his Nanny Keti.

Nanny Kitty with Lucas

About the Author:

Miriam Claire has taught singing, voice technique, movement and music to over 2000 children in Los Angeles and other countries. She taught the pre-school music program at Kirk O' The Valley School in Los Angeles for 6 years while her son was a student at the school. Bye-Bye Nanny is her first book for young children and she is the author of an acclaimed adult nonfiction book. Miriam lives in Los Angeles with both her human and furry family.

Printed in the United States
By Bookmasters